CASE STUDIES IN
ERISA:

Why It Matters And How It Benefits You

A Plan Sponsor's Guide To
Employee Benefits Legal Compliance

D1453561

ANNE TYLER HALL

Founding Attorney and Principal

DEDICATION

This book is dedicated to employers who recognize that strategically-designed, legally-compliant employee benefit plans are the cornerstone of long-term business stability and growth. It is also dedicated to the executives and HR professionals who work tirelessly to ensure their employees are provided with benefits and compensation commensurate with the long hours and sweat equity they provide the businesses that form the backbone of our American economy.

DISCLAIMER

For purposes of this publication, all defined terms are italicized. Whenever a gender-specific term is used, it should be understood as referring to both genders. This publication is intended to be used for educational purposes only. No legal advice is being given, and no attorney-client relationship is intended to be created by reading this material. The author assumes no liability for any errors or omissions or for how this book or its content is used or interpreted or for any consequences resulting directly or indirectly from the use of this book. For legal or any other advice, please consult an experienced ERISA attorney or an appropriate expert who is aware of the specific facts of your case and is knowledgeable of the law in your jurisdiction.

Hall Benefits Law
270 Carpenter Drive
Suite 325
Atlanta, GA 30328
www.hallbenefitslaw.com
(678) 439-6236

TESTIMONIALS

"Hall Benefits Law attorneys are experienced, knowledgeable and professional. Hall Benefits Law was able to solve an issue we had worked on for two years to transfer our 457(b) plan to a new plan provider. Their assistance was invaluable and now our employees are joining the plan for the first time in years now that we have the new plan provider. I highly recommend Hall Benefits Law and would use them in the future for any issues that may arise. They also provide invaluable training to their clients on all the new changes HR professionals need to know."

- Lisa

****

"Anne Tyler is great at interpreting the law. Her research and easy to understand documents are professional, organized, thorough and delivered in a timely manner. We appreciate her accessibility and willingness to offer suggestions and meet with our clients in person or via phone for meaningful discussions and getting answers quickly."

- Andy Weyenberg

****

"Hall Benefits Law assisted me with review, documentation, and a written opinion for a specific DOL situation. Anne Tyler is professional as well as personable, articulate, and knowledgeable on the subject for which I hired her. Working with someone who has personality and good communication skills is not necessarily a common attribute. Anne Tyler brings these attributes. The price for the work done, independent research as well as client presentation, was very fair and I would be happy to recommend Anne Tyler to any associate or colleague in need of her legal expertise."

- H.W. Youngblood

****

"I asked for the team at Hall Benefits Law to assist me in my efforts to put in a Non-Qualified, Executive Bonus Plan for four executives of a Non-Profit Organization. After inquiring with David Hall initially, I began working with others on their team. They were very attentive to my needs and the needs of the client and were prompt with a very good deliverable. I was very pleased with my experience of working with Hall Benefits Law and I definitely would recommend them."

- Jim Crone

****

"Working with Anne Tyler Hall was a pleasure. She helped me transition two underperforming and underutilized retirement plans into a 401(k) plan for my organization. Anne was essential in walking me through the process, ensuring I understood any and all liability, and prepared appropriate documentation. I don't think the transition would have been as successful or smooth without Anne Tyler Hall's expertise."

- Stephanie Hodge

****

TABLE OF CONTENTS

ABOUT THE BOOK - INTRODUCTION

This book is for the proactive business owner, the CEO who knows her highest and best use of time and talent is acting as her team's quarterback and not getting stuck "in the weeds." This book is for the CFO who knows, perhaps firsthand, the weighty difference between an ounce of prevention and pounds upon pounds of cure. This book is for the HR Director whose harried day doesn't allow for additional concerns related to retirement plan design or governance. This book is directed toward the CPAs, the business attorneys, the third-party administrators, and the benefits brokers who recognize the value of forming a team with other specialists to achieve the greatest good for a client.

ERISA. The acronym itself suggests simplicity, but businesses of all sizes struggle with legal compliance when it comes to the Employee Retirement Income Securities Act of 1974, as amended ("ERISA"). Over the past year, the team at Hall Benefits Law collectively cringed as multiple plan sponsors (employers) asked us whether ERISA legal compliance was actually important, citing the current Administration's seemingly more lax approach to benefits legal compliance. Specifically, they point out that in January of 2017, President Trump issued an Executive Order Minimizing the Economic Burden of the Patient Protection and Affordable Care Act Pending Repeal, an order that permits federal agencies to exercise authority to reduce the potential burdens of the Patient Protection and Affordable Care Act of 2010 ("ACA").[1] However, statistics from the Department of Labor (DOL) show that ERISA enforcement activity has *increased* in recent years and under the Trump administration!

Department of Labor Audits

DOL conducts thousands of audits of employee benefit retirement plans, focusing on violations of ERISA.

In past years, the DOL collected "recoveries" for benefit plans totaling:

o   2018: $1.6 billion (45 percent increase over 2017)
o   2017: $1.1 billion million (41 percent increase over 2016)
o   2016: $777.5 million

In 2018, DOL closed 1,329 civil investigations with 860 (64.7%) of those cases resulting in monetary penalties or other corrective action for plans

• For 2018, DOL civil investigations led to:

---

[1] *Minimizing the Economic Burden of the Patient Protection and Affordable Care Act Pending Repeal*, January 24, 2017 (Available at: https://www.federalregister.gov/documents/2017/01/24/2017-01799/minimizing-the-economic-burden-of-the-patient-protection-and-affordable-care-act-pending-repeal (last visited February 4, 2019)).

- o 268 criminal investigations
- o Indictment of 142 persons — including plan officials, corporate officers, and services providers – for crimes related to employee benefit plans

- For 2018, DOL's benefits advisors closed more than 170,000 inquiries and recovered $443.2 million in benefits on behalf of workers and their families through informal resolution of individual complaints. "These inquiries are a major source of enforcement leads."[2]

These statistics evidence that proactive ERISA legal compliance is more important than ever.

Complex Legal Compliance Issues Require Creative Solutions

When faced with a client's problem, the attorneys at Hall Benefits Law see before them an opportunity. While the law may be written in stone, there is no law against approaching every client matter with new eyes and seeking creative legal solutions to lift the plan sponsor client above the seemingly unending morass of code into a new plane of compliance and profitability. In the pages that follow, ERISA Attorney Anne Tyler Hall presents seven employee benefits matters she and her team encountered. The examples that follow demonstrate novel approaches and solutions to complex ERISA legal compliance issues related to executive compensation, health

---

[2] Fact Sheet, *EBSA Restores $1.6 Billion to Employee Benefit Plans, Participants and Beneficiaries* (*available at*: https://www.dol.gov/sites/default/files/ebsa/about-ebsa/our-activities/resource-center/fact-sheets/ebsa-monetary-results.pdf (last visited February 7, 2019)).

and welfare benefits, retirement plans, Employee Stock Ownership Plans (ESOPs), mergers and acquisitions, and health care reform. We hope that you, like the clients who encountered these issues, will find these solutions enlightening and move toward proactivity in the way you approach employee benefits legal compliance for your business. Can you afford not to?

— David Hall, Firm Manager

ABOUT THE AUTHOR

Prior to forming Hall Benefits Law in 2013, Anne Tyler Hall practiced ERISA and Employee Benefits law with Alston & Bird, LLP and King & Spalding, LLP, two of Atlanta's largest law firms.

As a business owner representing businesses, Anne Tyler understands first-hand the importance of strategically-designed, legally-compliant benefit plans aimed at attracting, motivating, and retaining top employees. She also understands the importance of responsive and timely legal compliance guidance to businesses who are in six and seven-figure Internal Revenue Service (IRS), DOL, or Department of Health and Human Services ("HHS") penalty situations.

Hall Benefits Law serves clients in 25 states and was recognized by the Law Firm 500 in 2018 as the fastest-growing ERISA law firm in the country.

Education

- Master of Laws in Taxation, with distinction, from Georgetown University Law Center
- Juris Doctor from the University of Alabama School of Law
- Master of Science in International Development from the University of Bath
- Bachelor of Science in Finance and Economics, magna cum laude, from Birmingham-Southern College

Representative Experience

- Led negotiation that reduced more than 80 percent of the original 401(k) retirement plan penalty assessment by the Department of Labor for a multinational telecommunication company.
- Drafted and implemented comprehensive deferred compensation program for global architecture firm based in Atlanta.
- Negotiated settlement with the IRS to address six-figure health plan design legal compliance issue on behalf of national eyewear company.
- Reviewed purchase agreement in stock transaction and advised parent company of its ERISA obligations with respect to providing long-term disability benefits to a legal employee of a recently-acquired subsidiary for multinational irrigation company.

Admitted to Practice

- Georgia, 2008
- Alabama, 2006
- United States District Court, Northern District of Georgia

ABOUT THE FIRM

A boutique ERISA law firm headquartered in Atlanta, GA, Hall Benefits Law operates under the core belief that strategically-designed, legally-compliant benefit plans are the cornerstone of long-term business stability and growth. The HBL Team's commitment to relationship-driven, proactive service of its clients' needs has made it the fastest-growing ERISA and Employee Benefits law firm in the country over a four-year span from 2014 to 2017 on the Law Firm 500. In addition to its proactive benefit plan design work, in 2018 alone the Firm secured more than $2,500,000 in IRS and DOL penalty abatements and avoidance for clients assessed benefit plan penalties.

CHAPTER 1

EXECUTIVE COMPENSATION

What is Executive Compensation?

Generally, executive compensation refers to the financial payments and non-monetary benefits provided to high level management in exchange for work performed on behalf of an organization. Executive compensation packages typically benefit C-Suite management such as corporate presidents, chief executive officers, chief financial officers, or highly compensated employees, such as vice presidents, managing directors, and other senior executives.

Executive compensation differs substantially from typical pay packages for hourly workers or salaried management and professionals because it is biased toward rewards for actual results that align with shareholder value. As a result, unlike most other employees' compensation, most of the executive pay is at-risk. If a company underperforms, executives typically receive a smaller fraction of their potential pay. Conversely, if a company and/or an executive satisfies or exceeds the annual objectives and performance goals, an executive compensation program gives executives the potential to earn substantially more.

Executive compensation is part of the bigger compensation package picture, based on the following factors:

- **Base Salary.** What are executives and managers with similar responsibilities in similar companies making?
- **Short-Term Incentives, such as bonuses.** Are these bonuses based on individual, department, or company performance?
- **Long-Term Incentives.** Is the company/executive best suited for a profit-sharing plan, stock options, or deferred compensation?
- **Benefits.** Do these include qualified retirement plans, vacation days, and insurance (health, dental, disability)?

How Does an Executive Compensation Program Benefit Your Company?

Outstanding leadership is often the key to creating a scalable, successful business. Recruiting and retaining great leadership are critical to a company's success, and a competitive executive compensation plan plays an important role in that process. Executives who are improperly compensated may not have the incentive to perform in the best interest of shareholders, which can become costly for those shareholders and the organization as a whole.

Because the DOL and IRS exercise jurisdiction over legal compliance of executive compensation programs, it is important that companies hire ERISA legal counsel who understand the importance of a strategic and properly designed executive compensation program and its impact on a company's long-term success. We often have clients who come to us with a specific executive compensation program in mind. However, when asked, these same companies have difficulty explaining how this particular program they have selected will help their company achieve its primary objectives.

At the onset of a client relationship involving executive compensation, Hall Benefits Law asks critical questions that facilitate the development of a long-term, cost-effective, strategic, and appropriate executive compensation plan program, including:

- What are the company's primary, specific short-term and long-term objectives?
- How is company performance measured:
  o Individual performance?
  o Loyalty to the company?
  o All of the above?
- What are the demographics of those who benefit from an executive compensation program?

Once the company answers these questions, we consider at least two alternative plan designs and discuss with the company the optimal executive compensation program to satisfy the company's short-and long-term objectives.

What is A Long-Term Incentive Plan (LTIP)?

An LTIP is an incentive plan designed to encourage loyalty to the company. It is typically a three to five-year vesting period (although some are extended for as long as ten years). That means that the employee does not receive a payout for at least three years from when the employee joined the plan. Whether an LTIP is designed to incentivize individual performance, company performance, or a combination of both, the goal is to encourage long-term growth of the company.

What is Deferred Compensation (DC)?

Deferred compensation is broadly interpreted to mean compensation earned in one year and paid out in a later year.

Certain severance plans, retirement plans, and equity arrangements may fall under the purview of Code Section 409A, which governs the timing and form of payment for deferred compensation. It was added to the Internal Revenue Code, effective for taxable years beginning on or after December 31, 2014, under the American Jobs Creation Act of 2004. It was enacted, in part, to prevent executives from accelerating payments under their deferred compensation plans before a company went bankrupt (e.g., the Enron debacle). It was also enacted because Congress perceived a history of tax-timing abuse.

Code Section 409A

Generally, deferred compensation plans subject to Internal Revenue Code of 1986, as amended (the "Code") Section 409A, a body of law with strict requirements concerning modification of plan terms (i.e., time and form of payment). Code Section 409A strictly regulates nonqualified deferred compensation paid by a "service recipient" (generally, the employer) to a "service provider" (generally, the executive or employee) by imposing a 20 percent excise tax plus interest (in addition to federal and state income tax) when certain of its operational rules (i.e., a payment acceleration) are violated.

Generally, Code Section 409A delineates two types of deferred compensation programs:

- An account balance plan that records each employee's deferred compensation account balance separately on the company's books. The amount an employee elects to defer is credited to his or her account, as are the related earnings. Included in this category are plans that allow a deferral much like that of a Code Section 401(k) plan but that allow executives to defer, in a nonqualified setting, compensation that would ordinarily be considered to exceed qualified plan limitations.

- A non-account balance plan that calculates benefits on some other basis than deferred principal plus accumulated earnings. An example of a non-account balance plan is a supplemental executive retirement plan (SERP) and plans that base benefits on formulas used in defined benefit plan designs.

In considering the issues enumerated above, placing them in the context of a client scenario should be helpful in understanding how different laws governing executive compensation interact in the real world.

CASE STUDY: DECONSTRUCTION AND REDESIGN OF THE EXECUTIVE COMPENSATION PROGRAM FOR A COMPANY WITH LONG-TERM GROWTH AND RETENTION OBJECTIVES

Client: A global firm based in the Southeast with more than 400 employees. It had an existing, but ineffective LTIP and deferred compensation (DC) plan. The LTIP was intended to incent company and individual performance (although the plan design was flawed, and it was not driving performance as the company intended). The DC plan was intended to provide certain executives to defer compensation in excess of amounts allowed to be contributed under the company's 401(k) plan.

Goal: To optimize long-term company performance by implementing an effective incentive plan

Plan: Deconstruct the existing long-term incentive plan (LTIP) and DC plan (that was not driving performance as they intended) and completely redesign the incentive compensation program to optimize long-term company performance.

Process: Firstly, Hall Benefits Law reviewed the alternatives for deconstructing the existing LTIP and deferred compensation plans without violating Code Section 409A. Hall Benefits Law then implemented an executive compensation program designed to accomplish the company's short and long-term objectives.

LTIP: Existing Plan Design Features

The following provides an overview of the company's existing LTIP design features:

1. The LTIP in place, a non-account balance plan, was designed as follows:

- A Committee selected eligible participants and established Company-wide performance goals.
- Participants were awarded synthetic (i.e., phantom) stock when the company satisfied certain performance goals.
- Initial payments for each goal were made only when:
  o the employee terminated employment;
  o the employee attained age 65; or
  o upon death, disability, or change in control of the company.
- A second payment occurred on the first anniversary of the initial payment.

2. The company found that LTIP participants disliked the payment triggers. For example, if a participant earns an LTIP award when he is age 40 and remains loyal to the company throughout his career, he could not obtain payment for the award until age 65 (or at termination of employment, death, or disability.) The company felt that the payment terms encouraged employees to leave the company solely to receive their LTIP award payment (amounts that totaled well in to six figures for certain participants).

3. With our guidance, the company decided that it wished to implement a different non-account balance design to drive specific company performance. However, termination of the company's existing LTIP would result in the following prohibitions pursuant to Code Section 409A:

- Prohibition on the company's payment of benefits from the terminated LTIP (other than payments made in accordance with plan terms) for 12 months after the date the plan was terminated; and
- Prohibition on the adoption of another non-account balance plan for three (3) years from the date of LTIP termination. Under Code Section 409A, an employer must not adopt a new similar type deferred compensation (i.e., non-account balance plan) within 36 months from the date the employer first took the board action needed to terminate the such plan irrevocably.

Because the company did not want to prolong the waiting period for adopting a non-account balance plan, we kept the existing LTIP intact. We then discussed two alternatives for handling the LTIP as follows:

- Merge the LTIP into the new plan (maintaining the original payment dates, which was the root of the plan redesign); or
- Freeze the LTIP (preventing participants from earning any additional benefits).

Ultimately, the company elected to freeze the LTIP. However, there were still Code Section 409A legal compliance issues to avoid, including:

- The appearance of any "substitution" (which we analyzed based upon facts and circumstances); and
- Any variation in time and form of payment under the LTIP, which would result in a plan failure.

New Deferred Compensation Program: Plan Design

Hall Benefits Law designed a new deferred compensation program, a non-account balance plan, to address the issues in the LTIP, namely the prohibition on payments until a termination of employment or attainment of age 65. The new deferred compensation program included:

- Two separate and distinct deferred compensation programs to accommodate different teams within the company and different performance objectives for each;
- More flexible payment events, including payment of half of the value of certain awards seven years after the initial award and the second half of the award upon termination of employment; and
- Various types of awards, including cash, deferral, and equity awards.

Executive Compensation Design Considerations:

- **Eligibility.** Who can/will participate in the plan – key or highly compensated employees?
- **Awards/Contributions.** What criteria will be used to determine executive award or contribution eligibility?
- **Vesting.** Cliff (i.e., full vesting at a specified date) or graded (partial vesting over a period of years)? Determined on an individual basis? Will participants automatically vest upon a change in control of the company or disability of the executive?
- **Special forfeiture.** Will awards be forfeitable (i.e., termination for cause – and conforming this definition with any already-existing employment agreement)?
- **Distributions.** What are the distributable events (i.e., disability, change in control, unforeseeable emergency)?
- **Plan Distribution Timeline.** Will the company pay according to a set schedule (i.e., 5 years) or one lump sum amount?

Pitfalls to Avoid in Executive Compensation Plan Design:

The following provides an overview of some of the pitfalls we advise our clients to consider—and avoid:

- Vesting periods that are too long (10-year vesting period is often perceived by employees as being out of reach);

- Performance metrics (company or individual) that are unlikely to be attained; and
- Large lump sum payments due in the same year (i.e., consider installment payments to stagger payments over a period of years) to cash flow problems for the company and tax implications for the executive.

Conclusion/Takeaway:

- Growing, competitive companies grapple with how to attract and retain top employees.
- Outstanding leadership is the key to creating a scalable, successful business. Executive compensation programs can be a powerful attraction and retention tool and, if properly designed, can help strategically drive company or individual performance (or both). Thoughtful plan design, however, is critical.
- Running afoul of the legal compliance requirements, specifically Code Section 409A, can be devastating for both the executive and company. Therefore, engaging ERISA counsel to advise on legal compliance, initially and on an ongoing basis, is important for avoiding stringent penalties.
- Companies should engage ERISA counsel who take the time up-front to discuss primary short-term and long-term objectives related to incentive compensation. Ideally, ERISA counsel is a partner to the company and devotes the time necessary to understand the unique aspects of the company and facilitates the implementation of a strategically-designed, legally-compliant executive compensation program.

CHAPTER 2

HEALTH & WELFARE BENEFITS

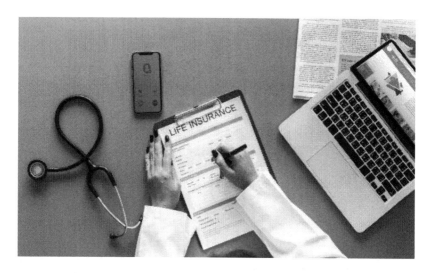

How Does ERISA Apply to Health and Welfare Plans?

The collective term "health and welfare benefits" generally refers to medical, dental, vision, disability, and life insurance. A "group health plan" is defined as "an employee welfare benefit plan established or maintained by an employer, an employee organization such as a union, or both, that provides medical care for participants or their dependents directly or through insurance, reimbursement, or otherwise."[3]

---

[3] ERISA § 3(1).

Most private sector health plans are strictly governed by ERISA which provides:

- Protection for participants and beneficiaries (participant rights); and
- The right to access to plan information.

In addition, the individuals who manage plans, and others involved in the administration of the plan, must meet certain standards of conduct under the fiduciary responsibilities specified in the law. Generally, the DOL, IRS, and HHS exercise governmental jurisdiction over the compliance of these plans.

Although ERISA was enacted in 1974, over the years many important amendments that apply specifically to health and welfare benefit plans have been added to ERISA:

- **Patient Protection and Affordable Care Act of 2010, as amended ("ACA").** The ACA, together with the Health Care and Education Reconciliation Act of 2010, represents one of the most significant regulatory overhauls to the U.S. healthcare system. The ACA, also referred to as Obamacare, was intended to expand health coverage and reduce the number of uninsured Americans, thereby alleviating the financial burden of those who could not afford health coverage.
- **Consolidated Omnibus Budget Reconciliation Act of 1985, as amended ("COBRA").** Prior to the enactment of COBRA, an employee who was terminated would no longer have healthcare coverage. COBRA was enacted to provide continuing healthcare coverage for a certain period of time to employees who voluntarily resigned or were let go for any other reason besides "gross misconduct."
- **Newborns' and Mothers' Health Protection Act of 1996, as amended ("Newborns' Act").** The Newborns' Act was enacted to provide certain protections relating to the length of hospital stays after childbirth for mothers and their newborns.

- **Health Insurance Portability and Accountability Act of 1996, as amended ("HIPAA").** HIPAA was added as an ERISA amendment to make health care information more secure and private for employees and their dependents.

Of the health and welfare benefit plan amendments to ERISA other than the ACA, the HIPAA requirements have proven the most far-reaching. Additionally, the penalties for noncompliance are significant. It is therefore incumbent upon companies, specifically those with 50 or more health plan participants, to engage ERISA counsel to aid in the development of a comprehensive HIPAA legal compliance program/model.

HIPAA mandates that all employers who offer health plans implement and adhere to a set of standards for the protection and confidentiality of individually identifiable health care information on electronic billing and other processes. HHS issued the Privacy Rule to implement the requirements of HIPAA. Within HHS, the Office for Civil Rights ("OCR") is responsible for implementing and enforcing the Privacy Rule for voluntary compliance activities and civil monetary penalties.

Protected Health Information

The Privacy Rule protects all *individually identifiable health information* held or transmitted by a *covered entity* (health plan and the administrator of the health plan) or its *business associate*, in any form or media, whether electronic, paper, or oral. The Privacy Rule calls this information *protected health information* (PHI).[4]

---

4 ¹45 C.F.R. § 160.103.

Individually identifiable health information is information, including demographic data, that relates to:

- the individual's past, present, or future physical or mental health or condition;
- the provision of health care to the individual;
- the past, present, or future payment for the provision of health care to the individual; or
- identifies the individual or for which there is a reasonable basis to believe it can be used to identify the individual.[5]

Individually identifiable health information includes many common identifiers (e.g., name, address, birth date, Social Security Number, etc.).

Who is Considered a Covered Entity?

The HIPAA Privacy Rule standards address the use and disclosure of individuals' PHI by organizations subject to the Privacy Rule (i.e., a *covered entity*). Such organizations include:

- **Health Plans.** Individual and group plans that provide or pay the cost of medical care are covered entities.[4] Health plans include health, dental, vision, and prescription drug insurers, health maintenance organizations (HMOs), Medicare, Medicaid, Medicare+Choice, Medicare supplement insurers, and long-term care insurers (excluding nursing home fixed-indemnity policies). Health plans also include employer-sponsored group health plans, government and church-sponsored health plans, and multi-employer health plans. There are exceptions—a group health plan with less than 50 participants that is administered solely by the employer that established and maintains the plan is not a *covered entity*.

---

[5] *Id.*

27

- **Health Care Providers.** Every health care provider, regardless of size, who electronically transmits health information in connection with certain transactions, is a *covered entity*. These transactions include claims, benefit eligibility inquiries, referral authorization requests, or other transactions for which HHS has established standards under the HIPAA Transactions Rule.
- **Health Care Clearinghouses.** These entities process nonstandard information they receive from another entity into a standard (i.e., standard format or data content) or vice versa. Health care clearinghouses include billing services, repricing companies, community health management information systems, and value-added networks and switches if these entities perform clearinghouse functions.[6]

Why is HIPAA Legal Compliance So Important?

OCR may impose a penalty on a *covered entity* for a failure to comply with a requirement of the Privacy Rule. Penalties vary significantly depending on factors such as:

- the date of the violation;
- whether the *covered entity* knew or should have known of the failure to comply; and
- whether the *covered entity's* failure to comply was due to willful neglect.

---

[6] This information was obtained from the HHS website at: https://www.hhs.gov/hipaa/for-professionals/privacy/laws-regulations/index.html

HIPAA penalties are distinct from most other ERISA penalties. This is because the OCR, in its enforcement of HIPAA penalties takes into account the level of the company's negligence regarding a HIPAA violation. For instance, if the *covered entity* was unaware of a HIPAA violation, and could not have avoided it, then the penalty is significantly lower. If the *covered entity* should have known, but could not have avoided the violation, the penalty increases. Willful neglect raises the penalty further. The penalties are issued per violation category with a maximum per year that the violation was allowed to persist.

The four categories used for the penalty structure are as follows:

- **Category 1:** A violation that the *covered entity* was unaware of but could not have realistically avoided had a reasonable amount of care been taken to abide by HIPAA Rules. $100 up to $50,000 per violation.
- **Category 2:** A violation that the *covered entity* should have been aware of but could not have avoided even with a reasonable amount of care (but falling short of willful neglect of HIPAA Rules). $1,000 per violation up to $50,000.
- **Category 3:** A violation suffered as a direct result of willful neglect of HIPAA Rules, in cases where an attempt was unsuccessfully made to correct the violation. $10,000 per violation up to $50,000.
- **Category 4:** A violation of HIPAA Rules constituting willful neglect, where no attempt has been made to correct the violation. $50,000 per violation.[7]

The maximum fine per violation category, per year, is $1,500,000. In addition, criminal penalties may be imposed if a person knowingly obtains or discloses individually identifiable health information in violation of the Privacy Rule. He may face a criminal penalty of up to $50,000 and up to one year of

---

[7] 45 CFR § 164.404.

imprisonment. The criminal penalties increase to $100,000 and up to five years imprisonment if the wrongful conduct involves false pretenses and increase to $250,000 and up to 10 years imprisonment if the wrongful conduct involves the intent to sell, transfer, or use identifiable health information.[8]

CASE STUDY: LARGE EMPLOYER WITH NO HIPAA COMPLIANCE LEGAL COMPLIANCE STANDARDS

Client: Manufacturing company with offices in five states across the U.S. and over 600 employees. The company sponsors a self-funded medical plan.

Goal: To create a formal process or procedure for handling the protected health information (PHI) of its health plan participants.

Plan: Design and implement a robust HIPAA legal compliance program to provide a roadmap for HIPAA decision-makers and mitigate exposure to costly penalties and fines.

Process: Hall Benefits Law designed and implemented a comprehensive HIPAA compliance program that included the following:

- HIPAA Policies and Procedures Manual
- Annual HIPAA Training
- Notice of HIPAA Privacy Practices
- *Business Associate* and Business Associate Subcontractor Agreements that follow HIPAA legal requirements

---

[8] *Summary of HIPAA Privacy Rule (available at:* https://www.hhs.gov/hipaa/for-professionals/privacy/laws-regulations/index.html (last visited March 5, 2019).

HIPAA Policies and Procedures Manual

To mitigate exposure to a HIPAA violation (and an associated costly penalty), Hall Benefits Law created a HIPAA Policies and Procedures Manual to provide a roadmap for HIPAA legal compliance. The manual includes the following guidance:

- A description of HIPAA's minimum necessary standard and associated requirements for health plans/plan sponsors
- A delineation of the HIPAA Privacy Rules, which govern the scope of permitted uses and disclosures of PHI by the plan sponsor. This section describes the explicit permitted uses and disclosures of PHI (as allowed under HIPAA)
- Participant's rights regarding PHI, including
  o Rights for restrictions on uses and disclosures
  o Amendment of PHI
- Communications with *business associates*
- Sanctions against employees who violate the privacy procedures
- Security safeguards
- Definition of and notification requirements in the event of a breach of PHI
- Electronic data interchange rules
- Description of requirements of the HIPAA compliance officer

HIPAA Training

Hall Benefits Law led HIPAA training that included explanations and practical application of the company's HIPAA Policies and Procedures Manual. The training, required for all employees with access to PHI, focused on the appropriate uses and disclosures of same. The annual training provides a refresher for those individuals previously involved in the handling of PHI and a primer for those individuals newly responsible for handling PHI.

Notice of HIPAA Privacy Practices

Hall Benefits Law drafted and implemented a notice for the client in accordance with the Privacy Rule that provided notice requirements related to privacy practices for certain participants. The notice contained information including a description of the ways in which the *covered entity* may use and disclose protected health information. The notice also described the *covered entity's* duties to protect privacy and abide by the terms of the Notice of Privacy Practices.

Business Associate Agreements

In addition to creating a Manual with a roadmap for HIPAA legal compliance, Hall Benefits Law drafted and implemented agreements with *business associates* of the company. Generally, HIPAA defines a *business associate* as:

- A person or entity who, on behalf of a *covered entity*, performs or assists in performing a plan, function, or activity that requires that person or entity to use or disclose protected health information. Such activities include, but are not limited to, claims processing or administration, data analysis or underwriting, consulting services; or
- Persons or entities performing legal, actuarial, accounting, consulting, data aggregation, management, administrative, or financial services to or for a *covered entity* where the performance of those services involves disclosure of individual identifiable health information by the *covered entity* (or *business associate*) to that person or entity.

Conclusion/Takeaway:

- Most health and welfare benefit plans are subject to ERISA, which means they are also subject to HIPAA, a federal law designed to improve the privacy and security of individuals' health information.

- To avoid significant HIPAA legal noncompliance penalties, companies should engage ERISA counsel to draft and implement a HIPAA legal compliance program that, at a minimum, includes a HIPAA Policies and Procedures Manual, HIPAA Notice of Privacy Practices, and HIPAA training.

- Annual HIPAA training is recommended; it provides a refresher for those individuals previously involved in the handling of PHI and a primer for those individuals newly responsible for handling PHI.

- A well-executed HIPAA legal compliance program can significantly mitigate exposure to seven-figure HIPAA noncompliance penalties.

CHAPTER 3

RETIREMENT PLANS

Why is Retirement Plan Legal Compliance So Important?

Like executive compensation programs, a retirement plan can be a valuable attraction, retention, and motivation tool for employees. However, for a company to maximize the benefits of a retirement plan, it must implement and maintain a legally-compliant program that is customized for its unique employee demographics.

ERISA establishes standards for retirement plans in the private industry. For example, ERISA specifies when an employee must be allowed to become a participant, how long an employee must work before he has a non-forfeitable interest in a benefit, and whether a participant's spouse has a right to be a part of the benefit in the event of the participant's death. The IRS and DOL exercise jurisdiction over retirement plan legal compliance.

Operational Errors Are Costly

Retirement plan noncompliance penalties are costly—and they are increasing! In an effort to maintain the deterrent effect of noncompliance, Congress enacted the Federal Civil Monetary Penalties Inflation Adjustment Act Improvements Act (Improvements Act) in November 2015 to require federal agencies to make a "catch-up" inflation adjustment. The catch-up increase, effective for penalties assessed on or after August 1, 2016, is capped at 150 percent of the November 2015 level. The following retirement plan legal noncompliance penalties generally apply for non-compliance issues occurring in 2018 and 2019:

ERISA RETIREMENT PLAN LEGAL COMPLIANCE ISSUE	2018 PENALTY	2019 PENALTY
Failure/Refusal to File Form 5500	$2,097	$2,140
Failure to provide documents and information requested by the DOL	$149 per day, not to exceed $1,496 per request	$152 per day not to exceed $1,527 per request
Failure to provide blackout notices	$133 per day	$136 per day
Failure to provide reports to certain former participants and beneficiaries and failure to maintain records	$28 per day	$29 per day
For plans with automatic contribution arrangements, penalties for failure to provide the required ERISA preemption notice to participants	$1,659 per day	$1,693 per day

The table above highlights some, but certainly not all, of the retirement plan legal noncompliance penalties. It underscores the litany of retirement plan legal compliance requirements, the costliness of noncompliance, and the need for ongoing ERISA counsel to advise plan sponsors on the numerous legal requirements to mitigate penalties.

As the Case Study outlines below, the issue faced by the client was manifold. For this retirement plan client, we evaluated the following:

- Use of a cash balance plan to increase tax-deferred retirement savings opportunities
- Increased advantages to cash balance plans under the 2017 Tax Act
- Plan design alternatives for avoiding Top-Heavy Plan status

Cash Balance Plan

Cash balance plans are classified as defined benefit plans. However, they share characteristics of both defined benefit and defined contribution plans. As in a traditional pension plan, cash balance plan participants are promised certain benefits at retirement. However, the promised benefit for a cash balance plan participant is stated as a 401(k)-type account balance instead of as a monthly income stream.

Under a cash balance plan, each participant's account balance grows annually based upon a contribution to the cash balance plan (a benefit credit) plus an interest credit. Generally, the benefit credit, as specified in the plan document, is either a percentage of pay or a flat dollar amount which is the actual amount an individual contributes to the cash balance plan. The interest credit is a guaranteed rate of return designated in the plan document typically tied to the federal long-term rates or set at a fixed percentage (generally 3-5%).

One of the primary advantages of a cash balance plan is the increased contribution limits. Because it is classified as a defined benefit plan, a cash balance plan is subject to higher defined

36

benefit plan limits. While a 401(k) plan participant is limited to total qualified retirement plan contributions of $56,000 (for 2019) (or, for 2019, $62,000 for those individuals age 50 and up), the maximum annual benefit that may be provided through a defined benefit plan is $225,000 (for 2019, subject to increases in future years for COLA). However, depending upon an individual's age and years of service with the company, a cash balance plan participant may be eligible to contribute two to five times the amount allowed under a traditional defined contribution/401(k) plan.

Any company considering a cash balance plan should carefully consider these points:

- **Administrative Time and Cost**. A cash balance plan is often costlier to administer than a traditional defined contribution or 401(k) plan. An actuary must be engaged to calculate permissible contribution amounts and certify plan funding each year. The employer and participants must be in a good cash-flow position to make required annual contributions.
- **Nondiscrimination Testing**. While a cash balance plan generally allows for significantly greater contributions (even for a highly compensated employee (HCE)), it is a qualified retirement plan and therefore must satisfy certain nondiscrimination testing requirements. A cash balance plan must cover the lesser of (i) 50 employees or (ii) 40 percent of the employer's employees. To satisfy nondiscrimination testing, an employer should plan to contribute between 5 to 7.5 percent of compensation to rank and file employees.
- **Participation**. Annual contributions are mandatory once they are established. Contribution levels can be modified via a plan amendment. However, frequent revision of contribution levels may draw IRS scrutiny. Therefore, the contribution rates should be carefully considered and designed to reflect a long-term strategy.

Companies that fall under one of the following categories are the ideal candidate for a cash balance plan:

- **Owners or partners who wish to contribute more than the defined contribution limit set by the IRS.** Many owners neglect retirement savings while they are building a business and often need a plan that allows them to rapidly accelerate pre-tax contributions to a retirement plan without the annual limit restrictions.
- **Companies that can afford to contribute for employees each year.** As outlined above, in order to satisfy applicable nondiscrimination testing requirements, the company is required to make contributions for staff as well.
- **Companies that have a reliable profit pattern.** A cash balance plan is a *defined benefit plan* with required annual contributions. Therefore, consistent profit is important.
- **Partners or owners who are over age 40 and desire to accelerate their retirement savings.** Contribution amounts allowed under a cash balance plan are age-dependent. An older participant can therefore contribute more to a cash balance plan.

Enhanced Retirement Plan Incentives: 2017 Tax Act

The Tax Cuts and Jobs Act of 2017 (the "2017 Tax Act") added a new Section 199A deduction for business owners beginning January 1, 2018. Generally, the deduction is equal to 20 percent of the taxpayer's *qualified business income (QBI)* from a partnership, S corporation, or sole proprietorship. *QBI* is defined as the income, gain, deduction, and loss with respect to the trade or business of the taxpayer. The QBI deduction applies to non-W-2 income (i.e., profits) only.

For specified service businesses (i.e., most professional firms), the 20 percent deduction is limited for owners with income of more than $315,000 (for 2018, married filing jointly) or $157,500 (for 2018, filing single). The QBI deduction is eliminated for owners with income of more than $415,000 (for 2018, married filing jointly) or $207,500 (for 2018, filing single). With the limitation on the QBI deduction for specified service businesses, taxpayers need deduction sources to reduce their taxable income. Consequently, tax qualified retirement plans, especially defined benefit plans (i.e., cash balance plans) that allow for significant annual contributions, represent a potential source of substantial tax deductions for taxpayers. While a cash balance plan (and other qualified retirement plans) was an attractive tax planning vehicle for many professional services firms prior to the 2017 Tax Act, they are now more advantageous than ever.

Top-Heavy Plan Status

A 401(k) plan is considered top-heavy generally when the total value of key employee plan accounts, on an annual valuation date, is more than 60 percent of the total value of the plan assets. If the 401(k) plan is top-heavy, the employer must contribute up to 3 percent of compensation for all non-key employees still employed on the last day of the plan year.

For purposes of top-heavy plan determination, a *key employee* is any employee who, at any time during the plan year, was:

- An officer making more than $180,000 in the current year (as of 2019 and adapted annually for cost of living adjustments (COLAs));
- A 5% owner of the business; or
- An employee owning more than 1% of the business and making in excess of $150,000 for the plan year.

CASE STUDY: RETIREMENT PLAN REDESIGN FOR RAPIDLY GROWING COMPANY

Client: A professional services organization with approximately 350 employees and approximately $100 million in retirement plan assets. The organization grew rapidly over the past decade—both organically and through acquisition.

Issue: Since 2009, the retirement plan assets had tripled. However, there had been no contemplation of whether the plan design still made sense for this rapidly growing firm. The plan allowed for little flexibility in plan contributions for certain participants (i.e., they were required to contribute a certain amount each year). Certain highly compensated employees wanted to contribute MORE to the plan while others desired to contribute less. Additionally, the plan had, in previous years, failed top-heavy testing.

Plan: Hall Benefits Law worked with the company to outline its primary objectives related to the individually-designed retirement plan. We determined that the following issues embodied the company's primary objectives:

- Redesign certain plan contribution requirements;
- Maximize tax savings for the company's leaders; and
- Avoid top-heavy plan status.

Plan Contribution Formula Redesign

One of the contribution formulas in the existing Plan required specific groups of HCEs to contribute to the maximum *Code Section 415 limit* ($56,000 for 2019). Some HCEs were frustrated that it was mandatory to contribute the required amount each year. These individuals had other, necessary expenses and wanted more flexibility in the contribution limit (i.e., the ability to contribute less than the current, required 415 limit). Other

HCEs had more flexibility in their budget and wanted to contribute more to the plan.

Hall Benefits Law identified several alternatives for easing the rigidity of the current required contribution plan design:

- *Revise the contribution formula to provide for a minimum and maximum contribution amount.* This allows HCEs who wish to contribute the maximum to do so. It also allows those with other expenses to cover (i.e., a child in college) to contribute less. At the same time, all participants are required to contribute something, because the employer was concerned that if participants were not required to contribute each year, some would not have enough saved for retirement when they reached normal retirement age.
- *Allow participants to waive their rights to the contribution.* The plan was drafted to position the contribution as an "employer" contribution. However, such contribution came directly out of the income of the participating employee. In our review, we noted that there was no prohibition on allowing a participant to "waive" his or her allocable share of this employer contribution.
- *Add a cash balance plan.* As part of the flexibility in plan design, Hall Benefits Law recommended that the company consider adding a cash balance plan to the existing 401(k) plan.
- *Adjust strategies to avoid the costly correction of top-heavy status.* Failure to satisfy top-heavy testing in prior years cost the employer an amount in excess of six figures in contribution adjustments to non-key employees. To increase participation and participation rates in the plan by rank-and-file employees the plan was adjusted as follows:
  - **Immediate eligibility to participate in pre-tax elective contributions for new hires**. The existing plan design allowed new hires to make pre-tax contributions only after completing one year of eligibility service. The new objective was to encourage rank-and-file employees to

41

participate in the plan earlier, creating a longer period in which to grow their account balances.

o **Automatic Enrollment Escalation.** The existing plan design provided for automatic enrollment at 2 percent contribution. We recommended the company automatically enroll employees at a higher percentage rate (i.e., 5 percent rather than 2 percent) with an auto-escalation clause each year until the participant achieved a 10 percent (or higher) contribution rate.

Because these plan design changes were significant, we recommended that the plan sponsor obtain an IRS determination letter approving the new plan design prior to implementation.

Conclusion/Takeaway

- There is a litany of retirement plan legal compliance requirements. Failure to comply with any of these requirements can be costly and time-consuming, which is why it is important to engage ERISA counsel to advise on a legally compliant model for retirement plan implementation and maintenance.
- As a best practice, and particularly as a company grows and employee demographics evolve, retirement plan design alternatives should be critically reviewed every three years (at a minimum) to ensure that the plan is optimized and designed to attract, retain, and motivate top employees and provide market features to employees.
- Operational issues, such as top-heavy status or nondiscrimination testing failures, should not be ignored as there are plan design alternatives (including executive compensation options) to address these issues. Plans should be designed to offer flexibility for a diverse employee demographic—providing the opportunity to contribute the maximum amounts to their plan for those who so desire and those with more restrictive budgets to contribute less.

- Cash balance plans can be an even more effective tax deferral retirement planning tool because cash balance plans are classified as *defined benefit plans* and are therefore allowed higher contribution limits. With the passage of the 2017 Tax Act and the allowance of a deduction from income for contributions to a qualified retirement plan, a cash balance plan should be a consideration for businesses with HCEs who fall under the highest marginal tax rates.

CHAPTER 4

FIDUCIARY EXPOSURE & ERISA LITIGATION

Fiduciary Legal Compliance: Avoiding Costly Fiduciary Breach Lawsuits

More than 6,300 class-action lawsuits were filed under ERISA in 2018.[9] For 2016 and 2017, the top ten ERISA settlements were $807.4 million and $927.8 million, respectively, and the top ten ERISA settlements totaled $313.4 million in 2018, for a three-year total of more than $2 billion. In 2017, ERISA settlements

---

[9] 15th Annual Edition of Workplace Class Action Report (available at: https://www.jdsupra.com/legalnews/15th-annual-workplace-class-action-12562/(last visited January 21, 2019)).

were nearly twice the amount of the total wage and hour claims and totaled far more than any other area of employment law.

Fiduciary breach lawsuits affect both small and large plans. During 2017, an excessive fee claim involved a retirement plan with only $3 million in plan assets and less than 20 participants.[10] In recent years, the largest ERISA settlements involved disputes over so-called church plans, breaches of fiduciary duty, general claims of retirement asset mismanagement, and failures to adequately fund pension plans. The following represents some of the most expensive 401(k) ERISA lawsuits in the last decade:

- Providence Health and Services (2017): $352 million
- Nationwide Life Insurance Co./Nationwide Financial Services (2014): $140 million
- Peabody Energy Company (2017): $75 million
- Lockheed Martin (2015): $62 million

Plaintiffs' attorneys continue to search for unwary retirement plan fiduciaries to sue. It is estimated that costs for a company to defend a fiduciary breach claim range from $500,000 to $750,000 but can be as expensive as $5 million (or more).[11]

Fiduciary Litigation Expands to Health Plans

Retirement-focused fiduciary breach lawsuits have proven lucrative. While plaintiffs' attorneys continue to target complacent fiduciaries of retirement plans, they have also discovered an

---

[10] *Goetz v. Voya Financial*, D. Del. No. 1:17-cv-01289-UNA, complaint filed 9/8/17.

[11] *Fiduciary Liability Claim Trends*, Lockton Companies, available at: http://www.lockton.com/whitepapers/Boeck_Fiduciary_Liability_Claim_Trends_Feb_2017.pdf (last visited January 21, 2019).

opening for fiduciary breach litigation against employer-sponsored health and welfare plans. With rapidly rising health care costs, more companies are collecting cost-sharing premiums from employees or becoming self-insured. This recent development has created a new target for ERISA fiduciary breach actions against unwary company health plan fiduciaries.

In November 2018,[12] a settlement was reached against the Carolinas HealthCare System (d/b/a Atrium Health ("Atrium")) related to provisions in its contracts with health insurers that restricted insurers from steering their members to lower-cost, high-quality providers. One of the key issues in the class action lawsuit was whether the company breached its fiduciary duty by failing to ensure that participants did not pay excessive fees for services, co-insurance, and deductibles by hiring a third-party health plan administrator (which was an affiliate of the company).

Plaintiffs' attorneys are now contending that employee premiums and pharmacy rebates are ERISA plan assets. Therefore, every decision regarding premiums and rebates is a fiduciary decision. If a health plan fiduciary is not carefully monitoring co-pays, types of coverage, pharmacy benefits, and premiums, he may have committed a fiduciary breach under theories developed pursuant to retirement plan litigation. The recent class action against health plan fiduciaries highlights the importance of establishing and documenting prudent fiduciary processes for making decisions not only on behalf of retirement plans, but also on behalf of health and welfare plans.

---

[12] *United States and State of North Carolina v. The Charlotte-Mecklenburg Hospital Authority, d/b/a/ Carolinas HealthCare System*, Civil Action No. 3:16-cv-00311-RJC-DCK (available at: https://www.justice.gov/opa/press-release/file/1111451/download (last visited January 21, 2019).

Who is A Benefit Plan Fiduciary?

There is a widespread misconception among benefit plan decision-makers that they are not responsible for the financial implications of their company's benefit plan. A recent survey shows that fiduciary awareness among retirement plan sponsors has deteriorated significantly over the past decade.[13]

- All of the survey participants automatically qualify as plan fiduciaries by definition, but nearly half (49%) of plan sponsors do not consider themselves fiduciaries.
- Among those plan sponsors who admitted to primary responsibility for the plan, one-third do not believe they are fiduciaries.
- About half the survey respondents indicate that while they have access to fiduciary training programs, they do not believe the training is comprehensive.
- 80% of respondents surveyed say their plans document the fiduciary process, but more than half of them express that the process could be improved.

These misconceptions and misalignments highlight the importance of engaging ERISA counsel to facilitate a better awareness and understanding of benefit plan fiduciary status and responsibilities, as well as to establish a fiduciary legal compliance program to mitigate significant exposure in this area. Being unaware of or not understanding fiduciary responsibilities does not lessen fiduciary liability.

---

[13] *New Research Finds Fiduciary Awareness Among Defined Contribution Plan Sponsors Continues to Slip*, Alliance Bernstein (available at: https://www.prnewswire.com/news-releases/new-research-finds-fiduciary-awareness-among-dc-plan-sponsors-continues-to-slip-300566567.html (last visited January 21, 2019).

ERISA 3(16) Fiduciary

An ERISA 3(16) *plan administrator* typically holds discretionary authority to administer the plan. A *plan administrator* is defined as (i) a person specifically named in the 401(k) Plan, or (ii) if a plan administrator is not named, the plan sponsor.[14]

ERISA 3(21) Fiduciary

A 401(k) plan's fiduciaries typically include the trustee, investment advisers, and any individual exercising discretion in the administration of the plan. A 401(k) plan sponsor may designate an investment committee to execute the fiduciary duties and help select contracts for 401(k) plan investments. Members of the 401(k) plan investment committee (including those who select investment committee officials) are plan fiduciaries. Additionally, any third party who renders investment advice for a fee or other compensation (direct or indirect) is an ERISA 3(21) fiduciary.[15] In the absence of an investment committee, any individual with authority to select 401(k) plan investments is also considered a 401(k) plan fiduciary.

The key to determine whether an individual or entity is a fiduciary depends on whether he exercises discretion or control over the 401(k) Plan.[16] For individuals involved in

---

[14] ERISA § 16(A).

[15] ERISA § 3(21)(A)(ii).

[16] DOL, Employee Benefits Security Administration, *Meeting Your Fiduciary Responsibilities*, available at: (https://www.dol.gov/sites/default/files/ebsa/about-ebsa/our-activities/resource-center/publications/meeting-your-fiduciary-responsibilities.pdf (last visited February 15, 2019).

benefit plan administration, an answer of "yes" to any of the following questions means that such individual is defined as a (ERISA 3(21)) fiduciary:

- Does one exercise any discretionary authority or discretionary control over management of the benefit plan?

- Does one have any discretionary authority or responsibility regarding administrating the benefit plan?

- Does one exercise any authority or control regarding the management or disposition of the 401(k) Plans' assets? [17]

What are a Fiduciary's Responsibilities?

ERISA sets forth a general standard of care that fiduciaries must follow to avoid liability. Under the *prudent man standard of care,* a 401(k) plan fiduciary must act in the best interest of the participants and beneficiaries and ensure that 401(k) plan assets are diversified, plan expenses are reasonable, and the terms of the plan and ERISA are followed. The following provides an overview of the fiduciary duties inherent in the prudent man standard of care:

- **Exclusive Benefit Duty.** A fiduciary must carry out his or her 401(k) plan duties solely in the interest of the participants and beneficiaries and for the exclusive purpose of: (i) providing benefits to participants and their beneficiaries, and (ii) covering reasonable expenses of administering the plan. [18]

---

[17] ERISA §3(21)(A)(i) and (iii). If a 401(k) Plan has a trust, the trustee is a fiduciary and should be named in the trust and/or plan document.

[18] ERISA § 404(a)(1)(A)(i)&(ii).

- **Prudent Expert Duty.** Under the prudent expert requirement, a 401(k) plan fiduciary must operate the plan in accordance with the care, skill, prudence, and diligence that a prudent man acting in a like capacity and familiar with such matters would use.[19]
- **Diversification Duty.** Under the plan investment diversification requirement, a 401(k) plan fiduciary must diversify investments with the aim of minimizing the risk of large losses. [20]
- **Plan Adherence Duty.** The plan adherence duty requires a 401(k) plan fiduciary to carry out his or her duties in accordance with all documents and instruments governing the plan (unless 401(k) plan terms are inconsistent with ERISA).

What are the Consequences of Failure to Comply with Fiduciary Responsibilities?

Fiduciary liability is personal, absolute, and unlimited.[21] A 401(k) plan fiduciary who breaches any of his or her ERISA responsibilities, obligations, or duties is personally liable to restore to the plan any losses resulting from such breach. A 401(k) plan fiduciary who breaches his or her responsibilities under ERISA may also be subject to such other relief as a court may deem appropriate, including removal of such fiduciary. For example, if an investment is not adequately diversified and a 401(k) plan fiduciary responsible for selecting the provider is found to have made imprudent investment choices, such fiduciary may be held personally liable for the losses to the participants and beneficiaries.

---

[19] ERISA § 404(a)(1)(B).

[20] ERISA § 404(a)(1)(C).

[21] ERISA § 409(a).

A 401(k) plan fiduciary's personal assets may be used to restore plan losses resulting from such breach.[22]

Establishment of Committee and Charter

Courts often refer to ERISA's standards as the highest standards to be found anywhere in American law. However, despite the demanding fiduciary responsibility that ERISA creates, ERISA itself does not provide much input regarding exactly how to ensure practical and effective fiduciary governance. As ERISA and its accompanying regulations continue to create new obligations for plan sponsors, the importance of a formalized, well organized fiduciary governance committee and committee charter are clear.

Fiduciary Liability versus an ERISA Fidelity Bond

There are two types of ERISA insurance to consider.

- The ERISA fidelity bond type of insurance only protects the plan against losses caused by acts of dishonesty or fraud (i.e., theft, forgery, embezzlement). Generally, retirement plan fidelity bond coverage must be at least 10 percent of plan assets up to a maximum bond amount of $500,000. It is unlawful for any employee benefits plan official to handle assets without being bonded.

- On the other hand, fiduciary liability insurance covers fiduciaries individually and is an integral component of fiduciary liability risk mitigation. The coverage level of fiduciary insurance varies widely. For example, if a fiduciary liability insurance policy in the amount of $1.5 million has a "deteriorating defense" clause, any amounts spent on litigation defense (i.e., $500,000) are subtracted from the coverage

---

[22] *Id.*

51

available under the policy for true fiduciary breach claims. In this example, only $1 million of the $1.5 million in coverage is available to protect the fiduciaries themselves.

CASE STUDY: DESIGN AND IMPLEMENT A FIDUCIARY LEGAL COMPLIANCE INFRASTRUCTURE

Client: A company based in the Midwest that handles billing for medical practices had a retirement plan with more than $50 million in plan assets. As the plan grew, and as fiduciary breach lawsuits against plan sponsors increased, the client was concerned about its fiduciary exposure.

Issue: Upon review of the company's retirement plan operations, we discovered that the plan had no processes or procedures in place for fiduciary decision-making.

Plan: To implement safeguards to protect the company and its retirement plan fiduciaries through education and design and implementation of a fiduciary legal compliance paradigm and ensure the fiduciaries were educated and adequately covered by insurance for any breach.

Process: As part of our ongoing fiduciary legal compliance review, Hall Benefits Law designed and implemented the following fiduciary legal compliance paradigm:

- A Committee Charter that provides a roadmap for Committee structure, membership, and Committee members' fiduciary responsibilities;
- Regular Committee Meetings (at least 3 times/year);
- Comprehensive review of Committee Meeting Minutes;
- Counsel and negotiation of fiduciary liability insurance coverage that provides maximum protection for the plan fiduciaries; and

- Counsel and negotiation of outsourcing a service provider of certain fiduciary responsibilities to a 3(16) designated plan administrator and a 3(38) investment manager.

Committee Charter

Hall Benefits Law implemented a Committee Charter to facilitate the establishment and ongoing process for a legally-compliant retirement plan committee. The Committee Charter included details for the following:

- A process for appointing Committee members;
- Fiduciary responsibilities of Committee members;
- Committee authority and purpose (including administrative and general functions of the Committee);
- Committee meetings, including constitution of a quorum; and
- The right to retain and rely upon ERISA legal counsel.

Fiduciary Liability Insurance

Our client erroneously believed it already had fiduciary liability insurance coverage and provided a copy of the plan fidelity bond which did not fully cover all ERISA penalties. When reviewing fiduciary liability insurance policies for our client, we searched for the most robust, affordable solution that included:

- Whether the policy includes coverage for certain other ERISA penalties;
- Whether our client is allowed to select their own defense counsel; and
- Whether the policy covers the costs of a Department of Labor audit or investigation.

Outsourcing Fiduciary Responsibility

For our client, we also reviewed alternatives for outsourcing some of its fiduciary exposure through a 3(16) designated plan administrator. While an ERISA plan fiduciary is never completely absolved from his or her fiduciary responsibilities and exposure to fiduciary liability, he can mitigate his exposure. Plan fiduciaries, however, still remain liable for the **prudent selection** of co-fiduciaries.

Conclusion/Takeaway:

- ERISA settlements (including fiduciary breach claims) totaled more than $2 billion from 2016 to 2018, highlighting the need for companies to retain ongoing ERISA fiduciary legal counsel to facilitate implementation of a strategically-designed and effective fiduciary legal compliance paradigm.
- Health plan fiduciaries should be wary of class action lawsuits filed against plan fiduciaries in 2018 that challenged fiduciary oversight and reasonableness of fees similar to actions against fiduciaries of retirement plans.
- While many benefit plan fiduciaries may not be aware of their fiduciary status or responsibilities, ERISA states that any individual with discretion over benefit plan assets, administration or management falls under the definition of a benefit plan fiduciary. Consequently, engagement of ERISA counsel to facilitate ongoing fiduciary training is a recommended best practice for mitigating fiduciary breach claims.
- As part of its fiduciary legal compliance paradigm, Hall Benefits Law recommends that a company with a benefit plan adopt, at minimum, the following four items:
  - o Committee Charter with a Committee that meets regularly;
  - o Review of Committee Meeting Minutes by ERISA counsel;
  - o Fiduciary liability insurance for each benefit plan fiduciary; and

- o Outsourcing of certain fiduciary responsibilities to other service providers.

CHAPTER 5

WHAT IS AN ESOP?

An Employee Stock Ownership Plan (ESOP) is a qualified defined contribution plan designed to invest primarily in employer stock. An ESOP allows companies to enjoy significant tax benefits while providing a retirement benefit for participating employees.[23] Most ESOP plans allow all full-time employees with one year or more of service to participate in the ESOP.

In general, employees do not contribute to the plan; rather, contributions are funded by the company as a benefit. Shares are allocated to employee accounts on a nondiscriminatory basis similar to a profit-sharing plan. ESOPs are primarily designed to invest in employer stock but can buy newly issued company shares or shares from exiting owners.

---

[23] *See generally* Code § 409(a).

In most cases, the company board appoints a trustee to act as the plan fiduciary. The trustee is often an outside trust institution or internal company manager who creates ESOP trust committees.

An ESOP may be the ideal benefit plan when the company wishes to:

- Buy the shares of a departing owner;
- Divest or acquire subsidiaries, buy back shares from the market, or restructure existing benefit plans;
- Purchase newly issued shares in the company with the borrowed funds available to buy new productive capital; or
- Attract and retain employees and create a benefit plan to share ownership broadly.

Usually when designing an ESOP, a company establishes an employee benefit trust, which it funds by:

- Contributing cash to buy company stock;
- Contributing shares directly; or
- Having the trust borrow money to buy stock, with the company making contributions to the plan to enable it to repay the loan.

Leveraged ESOP

In a *leveraged ESOP*, a company borrows money from a lender and loans it back to the ESOP. The ESOP then uses the money to buy company shares. The company makes tax-deductible contributions to the trust to enable it to repay the loan. The company can use the distributions of earnings (in an S Corporation) or the dividends paid on shares (in a C Corporation) to repay the loan. If the company is a C Corporation, these dividends are deductible. In 100% ESOP-owned S Corporations, there is no tax anyway, so deductions are not an issue. Effectively, the parallel loan structure allows the company to borrow money to acquire stock and, by channeling the loan through the ESOP, deduct both principal and interest. The company is allowed to use the proceeds from the loan for any legitimate business purpose. The stock is often placed in a "suspense account" and thereafter released to employee accounts as the loan is repaid.

Benefit of ESOP to the Company

If a company is sold to an outside party, the selling owner is responsible for paying taxes, which could be a significant amount if the sale is a cash transaction. Alternatively, the owner could sell the company through corporate redemption. This method is not tax-efficient either because the owner pays taxes and the company receives no tax deduction. An ESOP, however, offers considerable tax advantages to the owner and company.

An ESOP allows the company's contributions to pay for the buyout in an ESOP tax-deductible transaction. For example, a $5 million sale to an ESOP does not require the company to first earn this amount (or more) and then take the remainder (after taxes) to fund the buyout. With an ESOP, the funds used to buy out the owner are before-tax which is a significant advantage when compared to a traditional cash buyout. For a C Corporation, an owner can defer taxation indefinitely on the proceeds of the transaction by reinvesting them in securities of other U.S. companies and electing Code Section 1042 tax deferral. There is a separate tax advantage for S Corporations because the Code Section 1042 tax deferral is not applicable. For S Corporations, there is no federal tax, and often no state tax (depending upon the state) on corporate income attributable to the ESOP. This means that the S Corporation is not forced to pay distributions to fund tax bills if the ESOP owns 100 percent of the company.

Benefit of ESOP to the Owner

One of the primary reasons for selling a company to an ESOP is the ability to indefinitely postpone tax on the gains of the sale by electing Code Section 1042 tax-deferred rollover treatment. Generally, when an owner in a closely held corporation sells to an ESOP that owns 30 percent or more of the company, the seller can defer taxation indefinitely by rolling over the sales proceeds into stocks and bonds of U.S. companies. Additionally, if the selling owner holds the newly bought stock or bonds until death, there is a step-up in basis and his or her heirs will pay no capital gains tax. However, Code Section 1042 treatment is not automatic. The selling owner must formally elect the tax deferral and file the required paperwork.

ESOP Plan Design Considerations

The following are some of the primary ESOP plan design considerations for a company contemplating implementation of an ESOP:

- **Avoidance of a large repurchase liability**. The repurchase liability is usually affected by the distribution timing rules under the ESOP, the retirement ages of participants, the turnover of employees, and the rates of mortality and disability of participants. S-Corporations often establish reserves within a company because cash can be reserved by the company without being taxed on its savings if the ESOP is 100 percent owned. The following names three methods for funding repurchase obligations:
  o Accumulate cash in the Plan through dividends or S-Corporation dividends.
  o Maintain a sinking fund. A sinking fund allows the company to retain cash without it being taxed. It also allows the company to remain flexible about whether it

will contribute the funds to the ESOP to award (recirculate) shares or use the funds to purchase shares.
  o Corporate-owned life insurance (COLI).

Each of the above has implications to both the participants and the company and should be given careful consideration.

- **ESOP Cash Distribution Timing.** There are legal compliance requirements related to the timing and form of distributions from an ESOP. Pursuant to the Code,
  o Distribution must commence no later than the 60th day after the end of the plan year in which the latest of the following occurs:
    - Earlier of age 65 or the plan's normal retirement age
    - The 10th anniversary of the date on which the employee began participating in the plan
    - Termination of the participant's service;
  o Distributions on account of death, disability, and retirement must begin no later than the end of the plan year following such event; and
  o Distributions for terminations other than those listed above must be paid beginning with the sixth plan year after the plan year in which termination of the participant occurs.

The Code permits distributions to be paid either in lump sums, installments, or a combination of the two. Under the installment method, the Code allows for six installment payments over five years. For large account balances of at least $1,130,000 (for 2019, indexed annually), the Code permits up to five additional installments. An ESOP can provide for different distribution forms depending upon the reason for termination.

Contemplation of these types of plan design issues are critical to the success of an ESOP. An ESOP that permits immediate payouts upon termination can be disastrous for a company's cash flow. Therefore, the importance of engaging ERISA counsel to explain and consider long and short-term objectives of an ESOP as well as issues of concern cannot be understated.

Prohibitions on Concentration in Ownership: ESOPs and 409(p) Considerations

One issue to consider in the ESOP establishment is the avoidance of a disproportionate concentration of ESOP shares among a few individuals. Congress intended ESOPs to benefit the average company employee rather than a few highly compensated employees. To this end, Congress passed Code Section 409(p) which prevents abuses of the ESOP by limiting accumulation of ESOP ownership for employees who have reached certain ownership thresholds.[24] Section 409(p) only applies to S corporations with an ESOP,[25] and the statute prevents employees who are deemed to own more than 10 percent of the company individually ("Disqualified Persons") from collectively owning more than 50 percent of the ESOP.[26] Section 409(p) is violated when ESOP assets are allocated to Disqualified Persons during any year that Disqualified Persons aggregately own 50 percent or more of the S corporation equity (a "Non-allocation Year").[27] Upon violation of 409(p), affected employees incur a 50 percent excise tax on the disallowed allocation.[28]

Determining whether operation of an ESOP violates 409(p) is a multi-step process. First, Disqualified Persons are identified by calculating the percentage of all Deemed-Owned Shares held by eligible individuals. Then, the aggregate percentage of all Deemed-Owned Shares held by these Disqualified Persons is calculated. If the aggregate percentage owned is 50 percent or

---

[24] *See generally* Code § 409(p).

[25] Code § 409(p)(3)(A)(i).

[26] Code §§ 409(p)(3)(A)(ii) *and* 409(p)(4).

[27] Code § 409(p)(1).

[28] Code § 4979A(a).

more, the year is a *Non-allocation Year*.[29] Companies with concentrated ownership among one or a few individuals should engage ERISA counsel to perform an annual 409(p) analysis to prevent running afoul of these rules and the resulting significant excise tax implications to the affected executive(s).

Other ESOP Plan Design Considerations

When designing an ESOP, it is important to engage proactive ERISA counsel to determine whether—and which type—of ESOP is right for your company. In addition, the following plan design considerations can have a significant impact on a company's cash flow and volatility as it relates to each year's ESOP monetary obligations:

- Structuring Repurchase Liabilities;
- Releveraging (i.e., funding obligations paid by a new loan); and
- The vesting schedule

CASE STUDY: LEVERAGED ESOP FOR COMPANY WITH RETIRING OWNER

Client: A third party administrator (S Corporation), based in New York, whose Owner was retiring. The company wanted us to evaluate whether an ESOP was a good fit for succession planning.

Issue: The company's three primary objectives were to:

- Minimize tax consequences to the retiring owner;
- Allow employees to participate in the ownership of the company; and
- Maintain the company's good cash flow.

---

[29] Code § 409(p)(3)(A)(ii).

Resolution of the Issue: Hall Benefits Law recommended a leveraged ESOP for this client to mitigate cash outlay at the onset of ESOP implementation including:

- **Avoiding large repurchase liability.** Hall Benefits Law recommended maintenance of a sinking fund to mitigate exposure to a large repurchase liability.
- **ESOP cash distribution timing upon employee's termination of employment.** To maintain positive cash flow and provide adequate planning, we recommended that the company adopt the maximum delay in payment of ESOP awards upon termination of employment (except for death, disability, retirement, attainment of age 65, or 10 years of service with the company). The objective of this plan design alternative was to:
  - Avoid an incentive for participants to leave the company so they could liquidate their ESOP awards;
  - Offer continued incentive for terminated employees to support the company's long-term success so that they realized a higher value of their ESOP awards upon payout; and
  - Provide predictability and manageability of payouts for company budgeting.
- **Careful review of share ownership concentration to avoid 409(p) issues.** We recommended an annual 409(p) review to ascertain the status of Disqualified Persons and avoid a Non-allocation Year.

Conclusion/Takeaways

- An ESOP offers effective benefit plan alternatives for companies that wish to:
  - Attract, motivate, and retain employees by allowing them to share ownership broadly;
  - Buy out an owner of a company who wishes to exit the business, particularly from a tax efficiency standpoint for both the company and the owner;
  - Restructure existing benefit plans; or
  - Divest or acquire subsidiaries.
- A leveraged ESOP, or an ESOP where the company borrows money from a lender and reloans it to the ESOP, offers significant tax efficiency. Under this type of funding vehicle, the company makes tax-deductible contributions to the ESOP trust as part of the loan repayment. The company can then use the distributions of earnings (in an S Corporation) or the dividends paid on shares (in a C Corporation) to repay the loan.
- ESOP design should be carefully considered prior to implementation to avoid significant liabilities in one year that result in cash deficiencies for the company.
- It is best practice to engage ERISA counsel to discuss plan design options related to funding options for repurchase obligations (i.e., accumulation of cash in the plan through dividends, maintenance of a sinking fund, or corporate-owned life insurance) and ESOP cash distribution timing upon an employee's exit from the company. Companies with an ESOP should consider delayed payments of ESOP awards upon an employee's termination of employment to (i) deter an employee from terminating employment with the primary aim of receiving payment of his or her ESOP awards, and (ii) encourage terminated employees to remain invested in positive company performance to maximize the value of his or her ESOP awards upon payout.
- Finally, companies with an ESOP should engage ERISA counsel to perform annual Code Section 409(p) testing,

which evaluates ESOP ownership concentration. Failure to comply with these important rules can result in a significant excise tax (50 percent) on the payout of the affected executive's ESOP awards.

CHAPTER 6

EMPLOYEE BENEFITS IN CORPORATE TRANSACTIONS

Why is ERISA Legal Compliance Important in A Corporate Transaction?

Over the past several years, there has been a surge in corporate transaction opportunities or mergers and acquisitions (M&A). Companies involved in a buy or sell transaction must carefully consider a variety of ERISA legal compliance issues to avoid inheriting or creating the potential for substantial employee benefit plan liabilities.

As a best practice prior to a corporate transaction, both the buyer and seller should engage in due diligence before a deal closes to understand the types and designs of existing benefit plans. Due diligence includes a process of verification, investigation, or audit of a potential transaction to confirm all facts, financial information, and anything else that becomes apparent during the transaction investment process. Both buyer and seller should engage ERISA counsel to carefully review and negotiate the terms of the purchase agreement and take appropriate pre- and post-closing actions to mitigate exposure to any ERISA legal compliance problems. Failure to engage in these best practices can result in six and seven-figure unintended liabilities.

Stock versus Asset Purchase Transactions

Stock Acquisition

Whether the transaction is an asset purchase or stock purchase is a threshold issue that affects all employee benefit plan transaction activities. In a stock transaction, the buyer purchases the selling company and acquires ownership of the company's stock or other ownership interests. This type of transaction is best exemplified in the typical parent-subsidiary scenario where the purchasing entity owns at least 80 percent of the interests/stock of the seller's business entity. Subsequent to a stock acquisition, both the buyer's and seller's entities are typically part of the same "controlled group."

Controlled group status has significant implications related to retirement and health plans. Pursuant to IRS requirements, entities in the same controlled group are treated as one employer for purposes of retirement plan nondiscrimination testing. Therefore, retirement plan benefits for one entity in a controlled group cannot disproportionately favor highly compensated employees. The "one employer" controlled group rules also apply with respect to the determination of applicable large employer status under the ACA. Entities in the same controlled group are aggregated to determine whether they employ 50 or more full-time employees (and full-time equivalents) and are therefore subject to the Employer "Pay or Play" penalty under the

ACA. Buyers who fail to consider the controlled group rules and the implications of treatment as one employer may face significant penalties for failures related to retirement plan nondiscrimination testing and the applicable large employer health coverage requirements under the ACA.

In a stock purchase situation, the buyer assumes control of the employee benefit plans of the seller. Consequently, a stock transaction necessitates a greater level of scrutiny because the buyer assumes the liabilities associated with the seller's plans. The potential non-compliance penalties are significant for both large and smaller benefit plans acquired in a stock transaction. After the close of the transaction, the buyer — not the plan — is responsible for any non-compliance penalties. Therefore, the primary pre-closing objective for the buyer is identification of all employee benefit plans offered by the seller and any potential problems and liabilities related to those plans. Prior to close of the transaction, the buyer should engage ERISA counsel to help determine whether to integrate or terminate the seller's employee benefit plans.

Asset Transaction

In an asset purchase situation, the seller (or "target" company) generally remains intact but sells all or most of its assets to the buyer. For example, a seller in an asset deal may sell its equipment, intellectual property, and facilities. Employees of the seller cease to work for the seller after the close of an asset sale and may or may not be hired by the buyer. In an asset transaction, the buyer essentially assumes control over the seller's operations. With an asset purchase, the employee benefit plans (specifically, qualified plans) typically remain with the seller. Consequently, the scrutiny recommended in a stock transaction is unnecessary in an asset transaction because the buyer is not assuming the liabilities associated with seller's benefit plans.

Purchase Agreement

A purchase agreement is a legal document that records the conditions for the purchase and sale of a business. A mutually binding contract between the buyer and seller, the agreement includes terms and conditions such as the purchase consideration, payment mode, structure of sale, and even the termination clause in case of a default. It is critical that the purchase agreement be carefully and thoughtfully drafted by ERISA counsel (or, at a minimum, reviewed by ERISA counsel) to understand and thereby avoid significant liabilities.

Retirement Plans

In a stock transaction, with respect to the seller's retirement plan, the buyer must determine whether to:

- Continue the plan "as is" (the buyer maintains two separate plans);
- Terminate or freeze the seller's plan; or
- Merge the seller's plan into the buyer's plan.

While maintenance of the seller's plan and plan termination options require careful thought and attention, plan mergers involve a host of legal considerations described in more detail below.

Plan Merger Design Considerations

The buyer will typically merge retirement plans if it wishes to provide the same benefits to all its employees. The primary advantage of this approach is the elimination of duplicate expenses related to maintaining two plans. When merging defined contribution plans, there are inevitably many dissimilar provisions between the buyer's and seller's plans. Reviewing the provisions and features of each plan is imperative. While the plan sponsor may be legally obligated to preserve certain features pertaining to the accrued benefits from the acquired plan, it may also want to consider adding new features or revising existing ones. In addition, the surviving plan should be evaluated to consider participant demographics and preferences as well as incorporate features from each of the predecessor plans that together promote the best outcomes for the participants.

Protected Benefits

Prior to merging the buyer's and seller's plans, the plans' provisions must be compared to ensure that the merger does not violate the "anti-cutback" rules of Code Section 411(d)(6). The anti-cutback rules stipulate that protected benefits that have already accrued cannot be reduced or eliminated by an amendment or transfer. Common protected benefits include:

- Early retirement benefits; and
- Optional forms of benefit:
  o Payment schedule;
  o Payment timing;
  o Commencement of benefit; and
  o Medium of distribution (e.g., cash or in-kind).

Roth Deferrals and Other Changes

A challenge can arise if one of the merged plans offers Roth elective deferrals but the other plan does not. Alternatives for addressing this issue should be carefully reviewed and considered. Existing Roth assets must be transferred into the surviving plan, retaining any necessary protected benefits and information, to determine when the Roth assets satisfy the five-year holding period generally required for a qualified withdrawal.

Automatic Enrollment

If the surviving plan offers automatic enrollment, the plan sponsor must determine whether non-participating employees of the acquired plan are automatically enrolled during the merger. Consideration should also be given to "sweep" employees who are saving less than the default rate into the automatic enrollment program. When determining how to apply the automatic enrollment program during the merger, the employer who matches employee contributions must also calculate the additional cost incurred as a result.

Other Considerations

While it may be the most logical approach, buyers should be aware of the legal compliance issues related to 401(k) plan mergers. An acquired company's plan may taint the buyer's surviving plan if, in the years prior to the plan merger, the seller's plan did not comply with the myriad of procedural and operational compliance requirements. To prevent unexpected compliance issues, before undertaking a plan merger the acquiring company should perform an exhaustive review of the procedural and operational compliance of the seller's plan in the years prior to the acquisition. The following provides some (but not all) of the primary legal compliance pitfalls that can create problems for the buyer's 401(k) plan:

"Transition" Benefits for Certain Employees

A company-level transaction may result in providing transition benefits offered in the retirement plan for certain employees. For example, a purchase agreement may provide that the buyer will make an employer contribution on behalf of the acquired employees for a period of time. When a non-match employer contribution is provided to a select group, it is subject to nondiscrimination testing under Code Section 401(a)(4) to ensure it is nondiscriminatory.

Contract Review

Contracts with service providers – recordkeeper, trustee, and the issuer of a stable value fund (SVF) or guaranteed investment contract (GIC) – should be reviewed. It is important to identify if:

- Advance notice must be provided when terminating these contracts;
- Conversion or short-term redemption fees are assessed, and if so, who is responsible for these fees; or
- The plan merger involves the removal of a GIC or SVF from the investment lineup.

Special attention must be paid to these contracts to identify potential liquidity issues. Most contracts do not extend the right to immediate withdrawals at book value when full liquidation occurs as a result of merger activity.

Overview of Additional Retirement Plan Merger Considerations

- *Forfeiture account.* The plan sponsor must determine, in accordance with the plan document, the permissible uses of any remaining funds in the acquired plan's forfeiture account.
- *Outstanding loans.* If the surviving plan does not permit loans, or permits fewer loans outstanding than the acquired plan, the plan sponsor has the option to grandfather these loans when the plans are merged. If the acquisition results in a different pay frequency, the IRS permits reamortization of the loans to match the new pay frequency. Reamortizing loans will likely result in a change in the payment amounts, which the plan sponsor should clearly communicate to the affected participants.

Health and Welfare Benefits

Welfare benefit plans in a corporate transaction typically include medical, dental, life insurance, disability, and severance pay plans. One of the most significant challenges in a stock transaction is allowing employees of the seller to continue welfare benefit coverage uninterrupted by the transaction. This requires careful attention to the different types of health and welfare benefits coverage provided by the seller and the buyer.

If the transaction is a stock deal, the buyer should determine whether the seller has its own plans or whether the seller's employees obtain benefits from some other company in the seller's controlled group. If the plan is the target's own, it continues to be maintained by the target after the transaction. If the target's employees participate in a welfare benefit plan maintained by another company in the seller's controlled group, the buyer will have to make arrangements for the target's employees to participate in the buyer's plans as of the closing or create plans for the target that will be effective as of the closing. Seller's employees will obviously prefer plans that are at least equally generous in coverage as the seller's plans. However, there are no "protected benefits" requirements for welfare benefits.

Other health and welfare plan considerations in corporate transactions include:

- Are there any ongoing or past IRS, DOL, or HHS audits related to seller's health and welfare benefits?
- Has the seller timely filed Form 5500s for each of its health and welfare plans? If seller maintains a Wrap Plan, does it include all required ERISA legal compliance provisions?
- Have requisite COBRA and HIPAA notices been timely provided to health plan participants?

- If the seller's health plan is self-insured, does the seller have Section 105(h) nondiscrimination testing results confirming that the plan is not discriminatory?
- Does the seller sponsor any retiree medical benefit plans? If so, how will these be handled post-closing?

Executive Compensation

Corporate transactions include a wide variety of executive compensation issues. The ideal executive compensation due diligence goes beyond a simple review of the financial liabilities assumed and extends to improving the likelihood of long-term success. Strategically-designed executive compensation programs are powerful tools to help support the pre-close and integration process in a stock or asset transaction. Retaining top talent as part of an acquisition is usually critical in achieving strategic and financial goals, and it takes both a full understanding of past practices and an eye toward the future executive compensation strategy to realize the desired outcomes.

Pre-closing, the buyer must understand potential liabilities and compliance problems associated with terminating the seller's executive compensation programs. Post-closing, the buyer must facilitate a smooth transition for all participants involved. The following provides an overview of two primary executive compensation areas in which to focus these efforts:

Severance Plans and Agreements

Severance plans often provide enhanced payments if the executive's termination is related to a change in control, and many plans have provisions that allow for severance if the employee voluntarily terminates employment due to "good reason," the definition of which can be broad. The buyer needs to know the total potential cost associated with these plans and whether key talent can leave voluntarily and still receive severance.

Guaranteed Compensation in Employment Agreements

Employment agreements frequently include guarantees of certain salary levels, bonus targets, or other executive benefits and perquisites. These guarantees may cause issues related to internal equity or corporate governance. The buyer must determine whether it should assume such guarantees. If not, it may need to negotiate new employment terms with executives before the deal closes.

Other executive compensation considerations in corporate transactions include:

- Does the company sponsor any supplemental executive retirement plans (SERPs) or other nonqualified deferred compensation programs?
- Were timely "top hat" filings made by seller to the Department of Labor?
- If seller sponsors a severance plan or agreement, is it an ERISA plan? Is it subject to Code Section 409A?
- Do all bonus, incentive, retention, commission, equity, or change in control plans comply with Code Section 409A?

CASE STUDY: VERTICAL STOCK ACQUISITION BY A MANUFACTURING COMPANY

Client: A manufacturing company in Ohio acquired the stock of a one of its suppliers. The aim of our client was to provide the seller's employees with similar benefits to those being offered by the seller. At the same time, the buyer wished to limit its cost and exposure related to the seller's health and welfare benefits and executive compensation programs.

Issue: The acquisition raised three primary concerns:

- Legal compliance issues related to merging retirement plans;

- Requirement of parent company to provide long-term disability coverage for certain target company employees (estimated minimum liability equal to $250,000); and
- Payout of executive compensation for certain executives of seller without violating any Code Section 409A requirements.

Resolution of the Issue: Hall Benefits Law advised the buyer and prepared an ERISA legal compliance memo and timeline outlining primary ERISA legal compliance considerations to ensure that such requirements were understood by the buyer. The Memo also memorialized the buyer's adherence to these ERISA legal compliance requirements related to the retirement plan merger and termination of seller's health and welfare and executive compensation programs as follows:

- **Plan Merger.** Careful consideration was given to seller's plan design and integration of same into buyer's plan. For example, buyer's plan allowed for Roth contributions while seller's plan did not. To accommodate this, we amended Seller's plan to accept Roth contributions of seller's employees who rolled into buyer's retirement plan.
- **Long-Term Disability Claim.** Hall Benefits Law carefully drafted the purchase agreement to include wording that, under the employee benefits provisions, the buyer was not obligated to provide long-term disability coverage to a target company employee who did not otherwise qualify for coverage under the buyer's existing long-term disability plan policy.
- **Executive Compensation.** The seller held employment agreements with two executives (originally entered in 2013) for a 12-month period of time and automatically extended for an additional 12-month period unless terminated. The employment agreements provided that unless there was a breach or other non-performance issue, the agreement could only be terminated by mutual consent of the parties. The seller did not have the ability to terminate this agreement unilaterally without liability to the professionals. We negotiated a written

severance payout agreement to the employees — not deferred compensation — to incent these executives to terminate their employment agreements.

Conclusion/Takeaways

- Corporate transactions have differing implications for employee benefit plans depending upon whether the transaction is structured as an asset or stock acquisition. While both types of transactions have implications for employee benefit plans, a stock transaction necessitates more stringent review of the seller's employee benefit plans because the buyer assumes responsibility for the seller's plans. Prior to close of the transaction, it is important for the buyer to engage ERISA counsel to carefully review and understand potential problems and liabilities associated with the seller's benefit plans.
- In a stock transaction, buyer can terminate, maintain, or merge seller's retirement plan. If buyer merges seller's retirement plan, it must carefully consider issues related to:
  o Protected benefits (i.e., certain benefits cannot be eliminated during a plan year);
  o Plan design issues (i.e., whether seller's plan allows Roth contributions and automatic enrollment);
  o Existing service provider obligations (i.e., fees associated with early termination);
  o Treatment of outstanding loans; and
  o Providing transition benefits to seller's employees.
- While health and welfare benefits do not have "protected benefits" like qualified retirement plans, the seller's employees prefer that the buyer's health and welfare benefits closely mirror those offered by the seller. Consideration should be given to existing plans and liabilities as well as plan design issues upon the seller's employees' transfer to the buyer's health and welfare benefit plans.
- Executive payouts in a corporate transaction can be complicated and costly. It is important for the buyer to carefully review the

seller's executive compensation programs to facilitate an understanding of potential liabilities and problems prior to closing and provide context for strategic design of retention programs for those executives whom the buyer wishes to retain after close of the transaction.

CHAPTER 7

HEALTHCARE REFORM

Why is ACA Legal Compliance So Important?

The ACA is one of the greatest overhauls of the health care system in U.S. history. Upon its passage, it was estimated that it would extend health coverage to more than 94 percent of Americans. Along with the expansion of health coverage, the ACA included a variety of group health insurance reforms that were rolled out from 2011 – 2014, including:

- **Prohibition on pre-existing condition exclusions in health plans.** Insurance companies cannot deny coverage to individuals due to a pre-existing condition.
- **Extension of dependent coverage for young adults.** Young adults can stay on their parents' insurance until age 26, even if they are not full-time students. This extension applies to all new plans.

- **"First-dollar" prevention benefits.** All new health insurance policies must cover preventive care and pay a portion of all preventive care visits.
- **No lifetime limits on coverage.** This eliminates any maximum dollar amount that a health insurance company agrees to pay on behalf of a member for covered services during the course of his or her lifetime.

Individual Penalties

In addition to the reforms above, beginning in 2014 the ACA required all individuals to purchase health insurance or pay a penalty to prevent people from waiting until they got sick to buy health insurance. The penalties for failure to purchase health insurance increased as follows:

- In 2014, the penalty started at the greater of $95 for an adult or 1 percent of family income above the federal tax filing threshold;
- In 2015, the penalty was the greater of $325 or 2 percent of family income above the federal tax filing threshold; and
- In 2016, the penalty was the greater of $695 or 2.5 percent of family income above the federal tax filing threshold.

Under the 2017 Tax Act, the individual penalty was reduced to $0 beginning January 1, 2019, effectively eliminating the individual mandate penalty.

Employer Pay or Play Mandate

The ACA also implemented a penalty against *applicable large employers (ALEs)* who failed to offer employees ACA-compliant coverage. To avoid the ACA Employer 'Pay or Play' penalty, an employer must offer *minimum essential coverage (MEC)* in addition to health coverage that provides *minimum value* and is *affordable* to *substantially all* of its *full-time employees*. The penalty applies to *full-time employees* only (those who work 30 hours or more a week).

Employer Penalties

The employer shared responsibility provisions were first effective in 2015, but several forms of transition relief were available for 2015 and 2016. Beginning in 2015, an employer who fails to offer ACA-compliant health coverage to *substantially all* of its *full-time employees* (and their dependents) may be subject to a penalty under Code Section 4980H(a) (Penalty A) if at least one employee purchases health insurance on the Health Insurance Marketplace (the "Exchange") and is certified as being eligible for a premium tax credit or cost-sharing subsidy. Penalty A applies to all of the employer's *full-time employees* minus the first 30 (80 for 2015). If an employer is not subject to Penalty A, a penalty under Code Section 4980H(b) (Penalty B) may still apply. If an employer offers *minimum essential coverage* to *substantially all* of its *full-time employees* (and their dependents) but at least one *full-time employee* purchases health coverage on the Exchange and is certified as being allowed a premium tax credit because the coverage was unaffordable, did not provide minimum value, or the *full-time employee* was not offered coverage, Penalty B applies to the employer. However, the employer is responsible for Penalty B only with respect to those *full-time employees* who purchase insurance on the Exchange and are eligible for a premium tax credit or cost-sharing subsidy (versus Penalty A where the employer is assessed a penalty on all full-time employees minus the first 30). The following provides a summary of applicable Penalty A and B amounts for 2015-2019:

ACA "Pay or Play" Penalties

Year	2015	2016	2017	2018	2019
Penalty A per employee per year	$2080	$2160	$2260	$2320	$2500
Penalty B per employee per year	$3120	$3240	$3390	$3480	$3750

Variable Hour Employees

The IRS has provided guidelines to determine whether employees with fluctuating hours fall under the definition of a *full-time employee* for purposes of the ACA. Variable hour status is reserved for those employees whose work schedules fluctuate so greatly that there is no way of knowing, at date of hire, whether they should be classified as full or part-time employees. The IRS has audited variable hour status of large groups of employees to identify employers who misuse this status to avoid offering health coverage to an employee at date of hire.

Applicable Law: Definition of Variable Hour Employee

Under IRS guidance,[30] factors that determine whether an employee is reasonably expected to be employed on average at least 30 hours of service per week include, but are not limited to, whether:

---

[30] Treas. Reg. § 54.4980H-1(a)(49)(ii)(A)

- The employee is replacing an employee who was or was not a full-time employee;
- Employees in the same or comparable positions are or are not full-time employees; and
- The job was advertised or otherwise communicated to the new hire or otherwise documented (for example, through a contract or job description) as:
  - requiring 30 or more hours of service per week;
  - requiring less than 30 hours of service per week; or
  - a variation of the above, below an average of 30 hours of service per week.

Pursuant to IRS guidance, no single factor is determinative.

IRS Penalty Notice: Letter 226J

Beginning in 2017, the IRS issued Letter 226J to ALEs who were subject to penalties for a prior tax year related to the employer 'Pay or Play' mandate (Employer Shared Responsibility Payment (ESRP) Penalty). ALEs in receipt of Letter 226J are usually provided 30 days from the date of the letter to respond.

Letter 226J includes information on individual employees who, during the applicable plan year and for at least one month in that year:

- were *full-time employees;*
- were allowed a premium tax credit; and
- for whom the ALE did not qualify for an affordability safe harbor or other relief.

The letter contains a summary table itemizing the proposed payment by month and indicating for each month whether Penalty A or B applied.

It is recommended that an ALE in receipt of an IRS Letter 226J notice of penalty assessment proceed as follows:

- Immediately contact ERISA counsel to discuss the letter and develop a process for substantiating any disagreement with the IRS's ESRP Penalty;
- Work with ERISA counsel to respond to Letter 226J, disputing all or part of such assessment. The response should include supporting documentation to justify the disagreement. Review payroll, time and attendance, and HR data required for IRS ACA filings to ensure there are no inaccuracies. If errors are uncovered, correct them and identify a process to ensure the inaccuracies are caught in the future; and
- Implement a process to maintain documentation for future tax years. Companies should make certain that all documentation that may be required to respond to a future IRS inquiry or audit is readily available when needed.

According to the IRS, failure to respond to Letter 226J within the requisite 30-day time period may result in a significant penalty assessment and possibly an IRS audit.

CASE STUDY: MANUFACTURING COMPANY WITH LARGE NUMBER OF VARIABLE HOUR EMPLOYEES

Client: A manufacturing company based in California engaged our firm to review their legal compliance requirements under the ACA. The company employs, on average, 300-400 variable-hour employees. The following describes the circumstances of these variable-hour employees:

- These employees retain the right to reject an assignment due to their preference for a different work project location or facility.
- Once a variable-hour employee's assignment is complete, he may have a period of time during which no offer of temporary

placement is made. In such a case, the individual is permitted to seek employment outside of the company.

- The duration of employment for a variable-hour employee varies dramatically based upon the job assignment and unrelated entity to which the employee is assigned.
- Some of the variable hour positions provide a stated job duration, but the length of the variable-hour employee's employment is often shortened due to task completion or other business reasons (i.e., financial constraints).

During 2016, less than ten (10) percent of Temporary Placement Employees achieved *full-time employee* status (1,560 hours within a 12-consecutive month period). Approximately 38 percent of Temporary Placement Employees were employed by the company for a period of 13 weeks or less, and the majority of Temporary Placement Employees were employed six (6) months or less.

Issue: During fourth quarter 2017, the client received an IRS Letter 226J containing a seven-figure assessment against the employer for failure to offer health coverage to its variable-hour employees at the commencement of employment.

Resolution of the Issue: Prior to receipt of the Letter 226J, Hall Benefits Law created for the client a compliance paradigm that included Memos outlining IRS guidance and checklists to facilitate determining variable-hour employee status. As part of this paradigm, before placing an employee with an unrelated entity, the company completed a questionnaire for each employee to memorialize factors determinative of variable-hour employee status. This paradigm, along with the supporting documentation, was submitted to the IRS disputing its seven-figure proposed penalty assessment. The IRS subsequently issued a letter of non-assessment (i.e., the full penalty was avoided) to our client.

Conclusions/Takeaways:

- The ACA is one of the most significant overhauls of health care in the history of the U.S. This body of law made sweeping changes to health care, including the requirement that *applicable large employers* offer health coverage to *substantially all* of its *full-time employees*. ACA also made significant group health insurance reforms.

- The Employer "Pay or Play" penalty includes two types of penalties that increase each year. *Applicable large employers* that do not offer ACA-compliant health coverage to their *full-time employees* (and their dependents) may be subject to six and seven-figure penalties Employer Pay or Plan penalties.

- With respect to determining the status of *full-time employees*, the IRS provides guidance when an employer does not know, at date of hire, whether an employee is expected to work 30 hours or more per week. However, the IRS scrutinizes employers with a significant variable-hour employee workforce to determine whether this exception has been misapplied.

- The IRS began issuing Letter 226Js outlining notice of the intent to assess A and B penalties. In the event that an ALE receives an IRS Letter 226J, it is recommended that the company work with experienced ERISA counsel to dispute the proposed ACA penalty.

- **This case study highlights the importance of being proactive.** Hall Benefits Law drafted a comprehensive variable-hour employee paradigm, along with supporting documentation, **prior** to our client's receipt of the IRS's notice of proposed penalty assessment. The compliance paradigm and supporting documentation was instrumental in the IRS's determination to dismiss the proposed seven-figure penalty assessment.

GLOSSARY

Affordable means that the cost for self-only health coverage must not exceed the following percentages of the taxpayer's household income for the taxable year:
o   2014: 9.50 percent
o   2015: 9.56 percent
o   2016: 9.66 percent
o   2017: 9.69 percent
o   2018: 9.56 percent
o   2019: 9.86 percent

Applicable Large Employer means an employer who employs, on average, at least 50 *full-time employees* (including *full-time equivalents*) on business days during the preceding calendar year.

Full-time employee means, with respect to a calendar month, an employee who is employed an average of at least 30 hours of service per week with an employer or 130 hours of service a month.[31]

Full-time equivalent (FTE) means a combination of employees, each of whom individually is not employed on average at least 30 hours of service per week, but whom, in combination, are counted as the equivalent of a full-time employee.

Minimum Essential Coverage means, with respect to an eligible employer-sponsored plan, (i) group health insurance coverage offered by, or on behalf of, an employer to the employee that is neither (a) a governmental plan within the meaning of Section 2791(d)(8) of the Public Health Service Act (PHSA), (b) any other plan or coverage offered in the small or large group market within a State, or (c) a grandfathered health plan, as defined in Section

---

[31] Code § 4980H(c)(4); 79 Fed. Reg. 8544, 8553 (Feb. 12, 2014).

5000A(f)(1)(D), offered in a group market, or (2) a self-insured group health plan under which coverage is offered by, or on behalf of, an employer to the employee.

Minimum Value means a health plan's total share of allowed costs of benefits provided under the plan is at least 60 percent of those costs. Applicable Department of Health and Human Services ("HHS") regulations[32] define the percentage of the total allowed costs of benefits provided under a group health plan as:

- The anticipated covered medical spending for essential health benefits (EHB) coverage paid by a health plan by a standard population;
- Computed in accordance with the plan's cost sharing; and
- Divided by the total anticipated allowed charges for EHB coverage provided to the standard population.[33]

Substantially All means 95 percent (70 percent for 2015) or more of an employer's full-time employees or, if greater, five full-time employees.

---

[32] *See* 45 CFR 156.20.

[33] 45 CFR 156.145(c) provides that the standard population used to compute this percentage for MV reflects the population covered by typical self-insured group health plans.